1720
Jack Rackham, Anne Bonny and Mary Read tried for piracy; Rackham is hanged.

1689
William Kidd first recorded as member of buccaneer crew.

1670
Spain and England sign Treaty of Madrid, and buccaneering raids decline.

c.1700
Widespread use of Jolly Roger flags.

1803
Napoleonic Wars begin; privateering flourishes.

1662
Henry Morgan receives privateering commission.

1694
Henry Every leads mutiny aboard privateer and begins pirating career.

1775
Beginning of American Revolution; privateering flourishes.

1718
Blackbeard dies in battle.

1674
Henry Morgan is knighted.

Map of notorious pirates

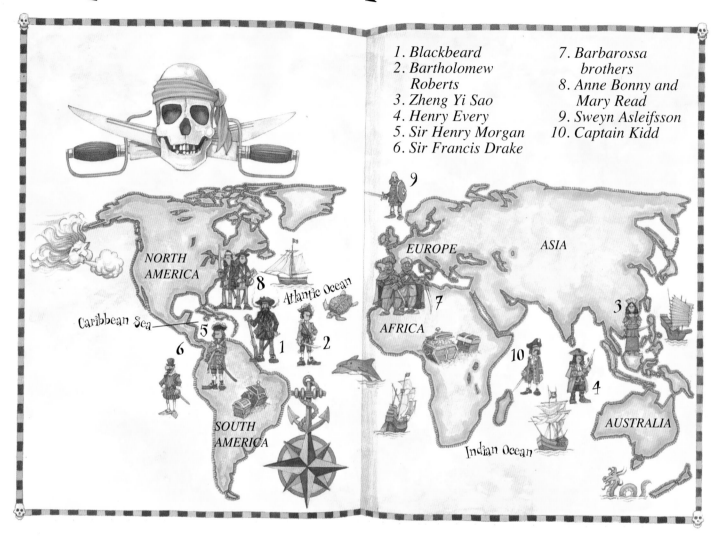

1. Blackbeard
2. Bartholomew Roberts
3. Zheng Yi Sao
4. Henry Every
5. Sir Henry Morgan
6. Sir Francis Drake
7. Barbarossa brothers
8. Anne Bonny and Mary Read
9. Sweyn Asleifsson
10. Captain Kidd

A world of danger

Ever since ships first sailed, pirates have attacked them. Pirate raids on ancient Egypt were reported almost 4,000 years ago. Greek and Roman pirates seized ships and passengers, Vikings looted Europe, and Chinese gangs terrorised Asian seas. These early pirates started a pattern of robbery and violence that continues today. This map shows where history's top ten worst pirates plundered and pillaged.

Pirate timeline

c.1470
Barbarossa brothers are born.

c.1540
Francis Drake is born.

1577
Queen Elizabeth I provides financial backing for pirate raids on Spanish ships.

c.1600
Rum invented by the Spanish in the Caribbean.

1500–1600
Increased trade between Asia and Europe attracts pirates.

c.1550
Spanish treasure ships become prime targets for piracy.

1596
Francis Drake dies of fever.

c.1655
Port Royal, Jamaica, becomes a haven for buccaneers.

Author:

John Malam studied ancient history and archaeology at the University of Birmingham. He then worked as an archaeologist at the Ironbridge Gorge Museum, Shropshire. He is now an author, specialising in non-fiction books for children. He lives in Cheshire with his wife and their two children.

Artist:

David Antram was born in Brighton, England, in 1958. He studied at Eastbourne College of Art and then worked in advertising for fifteen years before becoming a full-time artist. He has illustrated many children's non-fiction books.

Series Creator:

David Salariya was born in Dundee, Scotland. He has illustrated a wide range of books and has created and designed many new series for publishers both in the UK and overseas. In 1989, he established The Salariya Book Company. He lives in Brighton with his wife, illustrator Shirley Willis, and their son Jonathan.

Editors:

Karen Barker Smith
Stephanie Cole

Published in Great Britain in MMXIV by
Book House, an imprint of
The Salariya Book Company Ltd
25 Marlborough Place, Brighton BN1 1UB
www.salariya.com
www.book-house.co.uk

PB ISBN: 978-1-909645-71-4

SALARIYA

1 3 5 7 9 8 6 4 2

A CIP catalogue record for this book is available from the British Library.

Printed and bound in China.

Visit our website at www.book-house.co.uk
or go to www.salariya.com for **free** electronic versions of:
You Wouldn't Want to be an Egyptian Mummy!
You Wouldn't Want to be a Roman Gladiator!
You Wouldn't Want to be a Polar Explorer!
You Wouldn't Want to sail on a 19th-Century Whaling Ship!

PAPER FROM
SUSTAINABLE
FORESTS

You Wouldn't Want to Be™ a Pirate's Prisoner!

How did I get into this mess?!

Horrible Things You'd Rather Not Know

Written by
John Malam

Illustrated by
David Antram

Created and designed by
David Salariya

BOOK HOUSE
a SALARIYA *imprint*

Contents

Introduction

It is the year 1716 and the Caribbean Sea is the haunt of English pirates. These rogues are the menace of the Spanish Main – the area of land and sea between the northern coast of South America and the southern shores of North America. The pirates like to lie in wait for Spanish treasure ships. They are full of gold and valuables plundered from the peoples of the New World.

You are the captain of one of these ships. You hope to sail home safely to Spain, unseen by the scoundrels that lurk in these dangerous waters. To the pirates, your golden galleon is a great prize and, if they capture it, you wouldn't want to become a pirates' prisoner!

Treasure fleet! Your ship sets sail

In your ship's hold:

GOLD AND RICHES. At the port of Cartagena you collected gold, emeralds, pearls and valuable timber from the rainforests of South America.

VERA CRUZ.
At this port you stopped for porcelain, silk and spices from lands across the Pacific Ocean.

SUPPLIES. At Havana you took on board copper, food and water for the long voyage home.

X ou are the captain of a Spanish galleon. It is a large, slow ship with cannons and a hold full of precious cargo. Once a year you sail home to Spain from a port on the Spanish Main. You sail in convoy with many other galleons, all loaded with the treasures of the New World. There is safety in numbers and if a pirate attacks the fleet he's only likely to pick on one ship at a time. You hope it won't be yours!

SPANISH CAPTAIN. Dressed in your captain's clothes you are a grand sight. Your crew respect you and you are proud that your ship has never been attacked by pirates.

We are shipshape and ready to go!

Handy hint

Sail close to the warship that sails with the fleet – it's to protect you.

NORTH AMERICA

BAHAMAS

Vera Cruz

Havana

CUBA

CENTRAL AMERICA

JAMAICA

HISPANIOLA

Caribbean Sea

Cartagena

SOUTH AMERICA

WEST INDIES

N

W

E

S

THE FLEET. In the 1600s the Spanish treasure fleet sailed with as many as 90 galleons. Now, in the early 1700s, the fleet is smaller, with fewer than 12 ships.

Map of the Spanish Main in the 18th century

7

Pirates! Wolves of the sea

From privateer to pirate

Privateers were English, French and Dutch men who had permission from their governments to attack Spanish ships and territory in the New World. That has come to an end now, but some privateers are still up to their old tricks and steal for themselves as pirates.

English pirates have been attacking the Spanish treasure fleet for almost 200 years. Sometimes they raid ships while they are at anchor in port, taking them completely by surprise. Other times they take to the open sea, to look for a ship that has fallen behind the rest of the fleet. The first twenty years of the 18th century have been a good time for piracy in the Spanish Main and now there are more pirates here than ever before. They have turned many island ports into their own safe havens.

After

Before

NO MORE WAR. England and Holland were at war against France and Spain until 1714. Many sea captains fought as privateers, raiding Spanish ships. The end of the war has put them out of a job, so now they've turned to piracy.

Handy hint

Make sure the look-out stays awake on your galleon in case the pirates try a surprise attack.

Treasure ships ahoy, Cap'n!

PIRATE HAVEN. New Providence offers safety to pirate ships and their crews. It's a wild, lawless island, where hundreds of pirates are based – a perfect location from which to make a raid on a treasure ship.

Avast! Here be pirates!

THEIR SHIP. It is a sloop, a small lightweight vessel that cuts quickly through the water – perfect for surprise attacks.

Your ship sets sail with six others, all bound for Spain. But your galleon is so weighed down with loot that it can't keep up with the fleet. You fall behind and are on your own with no one to come to your aid if something happens.

A ship has been following the fleet at a distance and now it closes in on you. The ship raises its flag to identify itself – only then do you know you're about to be attacked by pirates! Their smaller, faster ship comes alongside and the English pirates are soon boarding your vessel to relieve you of its treasure.

PIRATE FLAG. The Jolly Roger is black with a human skull. It is designed to strike fear into your heart.

CAPTAIN. He's an outlaw who is known for getting exactly what he wants.

WEAPONS. They might be dressed in rags, but pirates are armed with a fearsome range of weapons.

Boarding axe

Flintlock pistol

Musket

Cutlass

Captured!

The pirate captain is not satisfied with pinching the loot from your ship. He wants the treasure from the rest of the fleet too. That is why you will come in useful. Now you are the pirates' prisoner, you are at their mercy. They want you to tell them what course the other treasure ships are taking. It's no use saying you don't know, because these ruffians know you do. Be warned – they have ways of making you talk!

So where be your fleet, then?

Rules of piracy

BOOTY. Your cargo of treasure now belongs to the pirates and it will be divided among them. The captain and the quartermaster will get double shares.

COMPENSATION. Pirates look after each other. An injured man will be cared for by his shipmates and he'll receive extra pay if he loses a limb.

Handy hint

Be friendly to the pirate captain. You never know, if he likes you, he might treat you like a fellow captain.

I'll never tell you!

FOOD AND DRINK. The pirates will help themselves to your ship's supplies. The food and drink will fill their bellies, not yours.

NO FIGHTING. The captain does not allow fighting on board his ship. Any arguments will be settled by a duel on shore.

NO GAMBLING. The pirate crew are not allowed to bet money on card or dice games on board ship. They must save their gambling for the tavern.

No escape! Your new home

The pirates will keep you in the ship's hold. You will be locked in this dark, rat-infested place day and night, ankle deep in filthy, stinking bilge-water, stale air filling your lungs. You will lose all sense of time and soon you won't know how long you've been down there.

You can forget any thoughts you have of escape. You cannot climb out of the hold and even if you could you wouldn't get very far. The pirates have fitted heavy iron shackles to your legs, which make it hard for you to move around. You have to get used to this life!

Your new shipmates

QUARTERMASTER. He is the ship's second-in-command who loves using a cat-o'-nine-tails.

SURGEON. He's quick with a saw, so if you injure a limb he'll have it off in no time.

CARPENTER. He mends the ship's timbers and his skill with a saw means he can do surgeons' work too!

SAILMAKER. He makes and mends the ship's sails and other canvas items such as covers and awnings.

NAVIGATOR. Using measuring instruments such as a backstaff, he plots a safe course for the ship to follow.

COOPER. He makes and repairs the ship's wooden barrels, which hold supplies of food and drink.

ORDINARY SEAMEN. They keep the ship in good order: swabbing the decks, manning the bilge pumps, working the sails, checking the rigging and so on.

Carpenter

Quartermaster

Surgeon

Navigator

Cooper

Sailmaker

Seaman

In irons! Shackled to the deck

A week of suffering

When the pirates eventually bring you up on deck, it's not because they're feeling sorry for you. Far from it – they are going to try and make you talk. To start with they'll clamp you in large, heavy leg irons called bilboes. There you'll stay, fastened to the deck for seven whole days. You will feel the full force of nature – the cold wind, the lashing rain, the blistering sun and spray from the salty sea.

Are you sure you don't want to tell the pirates where the rest of the fleet is?

MONDAY. You're taken from the hold and put in bilboes.

TUESDAY. You've had nothing to eat or drink for a day and a night.

WEDNESDAY. You're very thirsty, but don't drink the saltwater you're offered.

> Won't you help me, boy?

THURSDAY. There was a storm last night and the huge waves and movement of the ship make you feel dizzy and seasick.

Your wig

Handy hint

Lick rainwater from your skin and suck it from your clothes – it's the only fresh water you'll get this week.

FRIDAY. The sun beats down on your bald head all day so you get sunburnt.

I can't ! Cap'n would have me flogged!

Bilboes

SATURDAY. You're covered in blisters from the sun and salty wind and you're plagued by stinging, biting insects.

SUNDAY. You're thrown back into the hold with the rats and filthy water.

17

Flogged!
Cat-o'-nine-tails

So far, so good – you haven't told the pirates where the rest of the treasure fleet is, which means you haven't betrayed your fellow seamen. But now the pirates decide the fastest way to loosen your tongue is with a good old-fashioned flogging by the quartermaster with the dreaded cat-o'-nine-tails.

THE CAT is nine lengths of rope, each about 60 cm long, tied to a wooden or rope handle. Each of the 'tails' has three knots tied in it, covered in tar to make them hard and sharp.

FISH HOOKS. Some quartermasters are known to tie fish hooks at the end of the cat's tails.

Knots

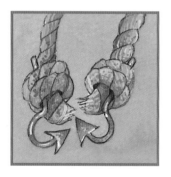

MUSKETBALLS. Some cat-o'-nine-tails have lead musketballs fixed to the tails for extra stinging power.

SALT 'N' VINEGAR. After the flogging you might have salt and vinegar rubbed into your wounds. It stings!

NEW SHIRT. Your back will be cut to ribbons – seamen call this 'wearing a checked shirt'.

As the quartermaster lets the cat out of the bag where it is kept, you are spreadeagled and tied by your wrists to a grill on deck. The pirate captain decides how many lashes you'll receive – it could be forty, fifty, sixty, or more. At the end of it, he will ask you the same questions once again. Will you give in and tell him, or not?

Handy hint

If you're told to make the cat for your own flogging, tie one knot in each of its tails instead of three.

Groan

Twenty-six...

Vinegar

Salt

Keelhauled! Man overboard!

Water torture

THE PIRATES have many ingenious ways of using the sea to punish you.

DUCKING. You might be suspended from a yard-arm and ducked into the ocean while the ship sails along. Hold your breath!

TOWING. You might be tied to the end of a rope and tossed into the ocean, then towed along behind the ship for hours.

You are incredibly brave! Despite everything the pirates have done, you haven't told them what they want to know. After the flogging they keep you in the ship's hold until the cuts on your back have healed – then they are ready for your next torture.

A rope is passed under the ship, from starboard to port. The pirates tie you to the rope and toss you overboard. You are about to be keelhauled – hauled by the rope, under the ship's keel. As your back scrapes along the ship's bottom, you'll be dragged over the razor-sharp barnacles that grow there. If you don't drown, you might die later from your wounds.

STITCHED UP. You might be sewn into a piece of old sailcloth with other prisoners and thrown overboard.

WEIGHED DOWN. You might be tied to a heavy weight, such as a dead body, then thrown overboard.

TARGET PRACTICE. You might become a target for the pirates to aim at. You'll just have to hope they're bad shots!

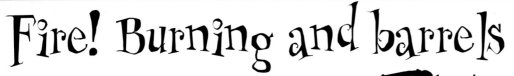

Fire! Burning and barrels

Feel the heat...

BURNING. Your arms and legs might be tied and pieces of burning rope stuffed between your fingers and toes.

The pirate ship has plenty of gunpowder on board but it is not just used to shoot cannonballs at other ships, as you will discover. Once again, the pirates drag you out of the hold and once again the captain demands to know where the treasure ships are. When you refuse to tell him, you are grabbed and bundled into a barrel filled with gunpowder. All it takes is one tiny spark to blast the barrel, and you, to smithereens! This could be your last chance to save your skin – before you lose it!

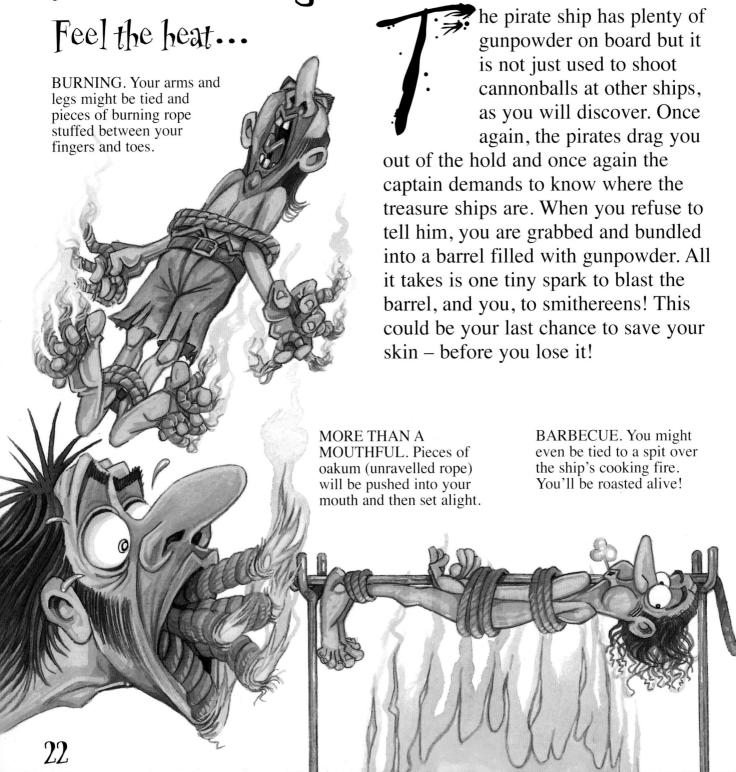

MORE THAN A MOUTHFUL. Pieces of oakum (unravelled rope) will be pushed into your mouth and then set alight.

BARBECUE. You might even be tied to a spit over the ship's cooking fire. You'll be roasted alive!

23

Diseased and done for

The gunpowder barrel is the last straw. The thought of being blown to bits is just too much so, as the fuse on the gunpowder is about to be lit, you break your silence. When you tell the pirate captain where the rest of the treasure ships are heading he decides to spare your pathetic life. Actually, he does it to save valuable gunpowder, but he wouldn't tell you that! Now you have to face up to a new danger: disease. You body is in poor condition and in your weakened state a deadly infection could set in. It would finish you off in no time at all.

I can't take any more!

Symptoms of sickness

SCURVY. You will have pale skin, your teeth will fall out, your legs will swell up and you'll have terrible diarrhoea.

YELLOW FEVER. Mosquitoes carry this horrible disease. You will feel extremely hot for days, then you'll either get better, or vomit black blood and die.

DYSENTERY. This will give you awful pains in the stomach and non-stop diarrhoea.

Handy hint

If you get scurvy, eat lemons, limes or oranges to make you feel better. (They're full of vitamin C, but you wouldn't know that.)

GANGRENE. If this serious infection sets in to one of your wounds, the surrounding flesh will quickly die. The ship's surgeon (or carpenter) might decide to chop off an infected limb.

Don't worry! It's only a BIT rusty!

25

Marooned – alone forever?

On a deserted island

The pirates have the information they need. You're not worth anything to them now and the last thing they want is for you to catch a deadly disease and pass it on to the rest of the crew. They decide to get rid of you by leaving you stranded and alone on a deserted island. This is called marooning and you have become a poor unfortunate marooner. From now on you'll have to look after yourself, living off whatever you can find on the island – at least you've seen the last of the pirates! Perhaps, one day, the long arm of the law will catch up with them and they'll get what they deserve.

CANNIBALS. You should hope you won't meet any – you might end up in their cooking pots!

GO MAD. With no one to talk to, you might lose track of time and you could end up losing your mind.

STARVE. If there is no fresh water or food, it'll be the end of you within a few days.

RESCUE. Keep a look out for ships on the horizon. Light a fire to let them know you're here and hope they come to your aid.

Handy hint

If you find footprints in the sand, take care! Their owner might not be friendly, especially if he's a hungry cannibal!

Now what?!

Saved! The Navy to the rescue

What happens to the pirates?

At last you have had some luck! The day after you were marooned, a passing ship saw the smoke from your fire and came to your rescue. Your saviours were the crew of an English warship of the King's Navy, sent to track down the pirates who have been robbing ships.

HUNG BY THE NECK. Captured pirates will be 'turned off the cart' – hung until they're dead.

HUNG IN CHAINS. An executed pirate will be bound in iron hoops and left to swing until his bones are picked clean.

HEADS OFF. The heads of executed pirates will be displayed for all to see.

PARDONED. Those forced into piracy and who have never used weapons against others are pardoned and set free by the court.

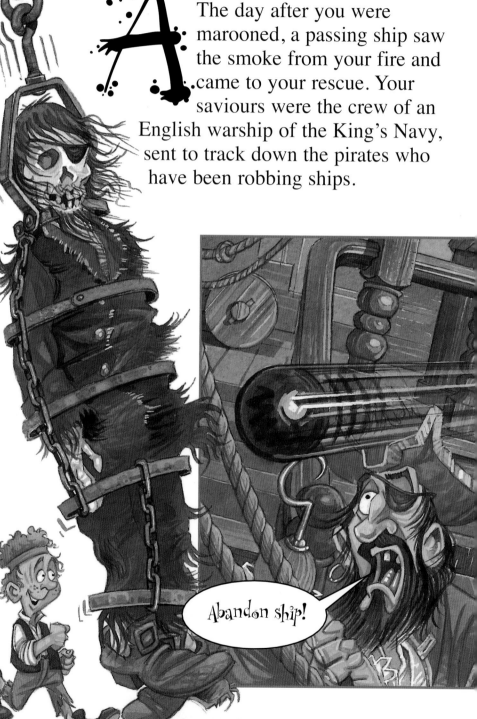

Abandon ship!

You have valuable information for the Navy captain about those who captured you and he easily hunts the pirates down. The pirate sloop is no match for the guns of the warship. The pirate captain and all his crew are taken prisoner. Eventually, you take command of a new ship. But you will not get your treasure back – the Navy ends up with it!

Handy hint

Clean yourself up, buy some nice new clothes and a new wig, ready to begin life as the captain of a new ship.

Argh! That was close!

Glossary

Avast! A seaman's command to stop doing something.

Backstaff An instrument for measuring the height of the sun in the sky. It was used by a ship's navigator to work out the position of the ship.

Barnacle A shelled animal that attaches itself to rocks and wooden objects.

Bilboes A bar with sliding iron shackles fixed to the deck of a ship.

Bilge-water Seawater that collects in the hold of a ship.

Booty Treasure and valuables taken by pirates.

Cannibal An animal that kills and eats its own kind.

Cargo The goods carried in a ship or other vehicle.

Convoy A fleet of vessels that travel together for safety.

Cutlass A heavy sword with a slightly curved blade and a basket-shaped guard to protect the hand.

Flintlock pistol A pistol that fires when a gunflint (a piece of stone) makes a spark that ignites a small charge of gunpowder.

Friction The action of one object rubbing against another.

Galleon A large, slow-moving and heavily armed ship designed to carry cargo.

Haven A place of safety.

Hold The inside of a ship, where cargo is stored.

Jolly Roger The name of the flag flown by a pirate ship. Its name may have come from an old English word 'roger', meaning a beggar or the Devil, who was called 'Old Roger'.

Keel The timber that runs along the bottom of a ship and forms its backbone.

Musket A gun that fires a ball of lead.

New World A European name for North and South America.

Oakum A substance made from unravelled old rope. It was used to fill cracks in a ship's timbers.

Porcelain A white, hard, shell-like material like pottery, made of clay and rock.

Port The left side of a ship.

Prize A ship captured by pirates.

Rogue A dishonest or troublesome person.

Scurvy A disease caused by a lack of vitamins in the diet, particularly vitamin C.

Starboard The right side of a ship.

Yard-arm The end of a yard, which was the large beam to which a ship's sails were fixed.

Index

Facts about pirates

Sailing! Robbing! Fighting!

Pirate life was brutal and bloody. Why did men – and women – choose such a risky career? Many were criminals or adventurers. For them, the sea was a place to hide or find freedom. Some were traders and explorers; a few fought for their religion. Most importantly, pirates wanted treasure. Stolen gold could make an ordinary crewman as rich as a king.

Swashbuckling pirates!

Yo ho ho! Most of us have enjoyed exciting pirate movies, set in exotic locations and featuring handsome heroes. Pirates in books and films are brave, romantic and glamorous. They fight for noble causes. They are heroes – and nothing like real pirates who lived long ago!

Did you know?

- The *Ganj-i-Sawai* was the richest prize ever captured by a pirate. A huge dhow (cargo ship) with valuable guns, she carried priceless pearls, precious stones, and half a million coins of solid gold and silver, as well as other treasures – including a saddle encrusted with real rubies!
- Either Henry Every or Emanuel Wynne may have been the first to fly the skull and crossbones flag. Sometimes called the Jolly Roger, this was a sign that pirates would show no mercy. So was a plain red *Jolie Rouge* ('pretty red') flag.
- Captain Bartholomew Roberts always put on his best clothes before a battle: a velvet suit and a shirt trimmed with lace. Proud of his captain's rank, he wanted to encourage his men – and face death looking good.
- Before battle, Blackbeard put lighted gun fuses under his hat. They surrounded him with devilish smoke. He also carried six loaded pistols.
- Viking pirates grabbed anything they could sell: gold and silver from churches, furs and amber from traders, and young men and women to be slaves.

Top notorious pirates

Captain Kidd British privateer William Kidd was licensed to attack both the French and pirates. In 1698, he captured the magnificent *Quedah Merchant*. It flew a French flag but came from India. Furious Indian princes accused Kidd of piracy, and the English agreed with the accusation. Kidd's crew deserted him and he sailed away to North America, hoping to find protection or prove his innocence there.

Anne Bonny and Mary Read 'Women are trouble!' That's what pirate captains said, and most sailors agreed with them. They complained that females brought bad luck or made crewmen jealous and argumentative. People thought that women could not fight or sail a ship – and everyone was amazed when two particularly cruel, clever pirates turned out to be women!

Henry Every A lifelong sailor, Every first went to sea as a boy on English navy ships. Seeking a quick fortune, he became a slave trader in West Africa, enslaving the merchants who sold slaves to him. Popular and a born leader, he became a pirate after leading a mutiny against an English captain. Then he headed far east, where he had a huge stroke of luck. He captured the Mughal emperor's ship, the *Ganj-i-Sawai*, which was filled with fabulous treasures.

Sir Henry Morgan The Spanish Main was a very dangerous place. But young Henry Morgan went there, eager to win fame and fortune by fighting against Spain. He led shiploads of savage buccaneers on secret English missions to attack Spanish settlements. In 1671, he destroyed Panama, a peaceful Spanish city, and was sent home in disgrace. But England needed his skills and knowledge, so he was pardoned and ended his career as governor of Jamaica.

Sir Francis Drake Master mariner, royal favourite and world explorer, Drake rose from humble origins to become England's national hero. Raised on a houseboat, he learnt seafaring skills from his uncle, a ruthless slave trader. Proud nobles despised Drake, but his courage helped defeat the Spanish Armada in 1588. And his privateering exploits raked in fabulous riches.

The Barbarossa Brothers The Barbary Coast of North Africa was home to a wealthy, elegant Muslim civilisation. But most Europeans did not know or care. They simply feared Barbary pirates! The most famous and successful, Horuk and Hayreddin Barbarossa, won wars against Christian Spain, conquered kingdoms for Turkey, and helped thousands of Muslim refugees escape to safety. Hayreddin also commanded the Turkish navy.

Blackbeard Most pirates were murderers. But Blackbeard chose a different way to win treasure. He behaved like a 'fury from hell' to terrify sailors. This, plus the 40 cannons on his ship, forced victims to surrender. Blackbeard captured a rival pirate fleet, took control of Charleston port (now in South Carolina, USA), and then began new adventures. British Navy ships

cornered him. He received five gunshot wounds and 20 sword cuts before collapsing.

Sweyn Asleifsson Good friends, a fertile farm, a big house, and a fine family – Sweyn Asleifsson had everything! How did he get it? Mostly by fighting, looting and killing! Sweyn was a typical Viking pirate. He fought to win fame and glory, to protect his family from bloody feuds, to win riches, and – according to Viking poets – simply because he enjoyed it.